Attack on America

Pancho Villa's raid on Columbus, New Mexico

Willie Ortiz

ISBN-13:
978-1535189354

ISBN-10:
1535189355

ACKNOWLEDGMENTS

I would like to thank my wife Sharon Ortiz for her constant support in everything I do and her never-ending love for me.

To my wonderful parents who always support me in everything I do and taught me anything is possible.

To my mother in-law Mary Hoolan, who has been a tremendous help in the process of making this book.

To Andy Lee for his knowledge of Pancho Villa and his men.

To Marcus Delgado thanks for the stories about your great great grandfather Papa Julio, who rode with Pancho Villa during his younger days.

Intersection at the beginning of town Columbus, NM

On March 9, 1916 Columbus, New Mexico had a population of 400 people. At 2:00 am on that morning, General Pancho Villa and his army of about 1,500 men cut the border fence about two and a half miles west of the crossing to Palomas, NM. Wearing their traditional crossed bandoliers and high crowned sombreros, the Villistas on their horses with the cover of darkness, they headed across the desert floor to the north into Columbus, NM.

View of Columbus from Cootes Hill

Less than a mile from the community, Villa gathered his troops and issued orders to his officers (Dorados). The Dorados plan was to lead their men to several strategic positions. From there, they would attack and converge on Columbus, New Mexico's businesses and on Camp Furlong. Villa would wait with reserves near Cootes Hill. Some of his men remounted. Others prepared to move forward on foot. In the pre-dawn darkness, a little after 4:00 am, he said, *Váyanse adelante, muchachos!* ("Go get 'em, boys!"), setting the stage for battle.

Timeline of the Raid on Columbus New Mexico

4:15am Two columns of Villistas simultaneously attack the center of Columbus and Camp Furlong.

4:30am Lt. Lucas awakens and calls his machine gun troops to action. Private Fred Griffin the sentinel on-duty challenges Villa's men and is killed but not before killing three of the Villistas before he died. Villistas loot stores on Main Street and assault guests at the Commercial Hotel. Lt James Castleman Officer of the day kills a Mexican rifleman at close range and leads his F-troop unit into the center of town from the east.
The Commercial Hotel bursts into flames lighting up the streets of the town. Lt. Lucas's machine gun troop and thirty riflemen disperse the raiders from the camp and advance on the center of town from the south.

5:30 am dawn breaks and Col. Slocum arrives at Cootes Hill to take command of the American troops.

7:15am most of the raiders are driven from town.

7:30 am the last of the Villistas retreat while General Villa and his reserves provide cover from a ridge to the southeast, Major Frank Tompkins and 56 mounted cavalry chase the Villistas a short distance across the Mexican border. The raid is over!

In total ten civilians were killed, eight soldiers killed, two civilians wounded, and six soldiers wounded. A total of eighteen dead and eight wounded. General Villa lost sixty-seven men.

Another view of the desert leading to Columbus, NM as viewed from Cootes Hill

Railroad pumper Milton James tried to help his pregnant wife from their home to the Hoover Hotel, which offered the protection of thick adobe walls. She took a bullet that killed both her and her unborn child.

View of Columbus, NM from Cootes Hill

Mrs. Parks, a telephone switchboard operator, stayed at her post and notified the world that Columbus had come under attack. She suffered cuts from shattering glass, but survived.

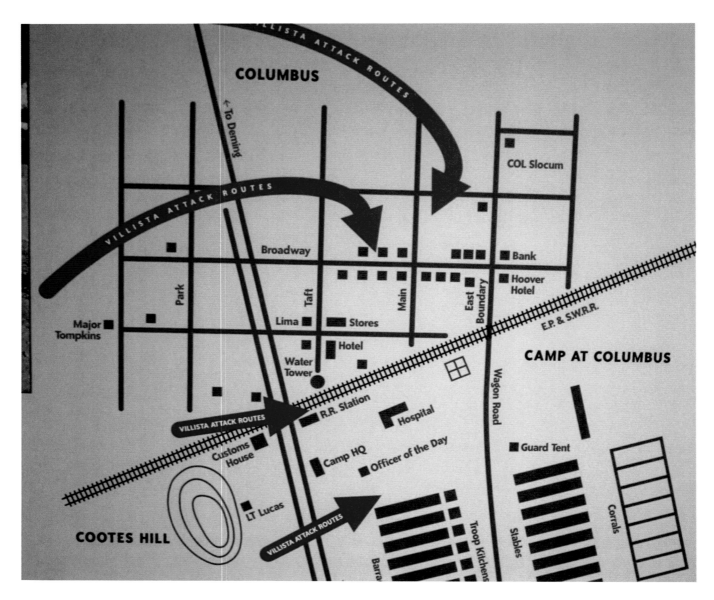

Mrs. Frost loaded her three-month-old baby and dragged her wounded husband into their car, and she drove her family north, out of the range of the gunfire, toward the town of Deming and safety.

Cootes Hill

Looking toward the southwest at military tents.

Home of Lt. John Lucas, Commander of the camp's Machine-gun Troop.

What is now Hwy. 11

U.S. Customs House built in 1902.

El Paso & Southwestern Railroad (now Hwy 9).

View of Columbus, New Mexico.

Mrs. Smyser, wife of one of the 13th Cavalry's officers, and two children climbed out a window of her home to the sound of pounding on her front door, and they first hid in an outhouse then raced through cacti thorns and nettles and into the desert.

Railroad Depot

  Why did Pancho Villa choose Columbus, NM? That is still a topic for debate among historians. The town had a garrison of about 600 soldiers. It was the home of Sam Ravel, a man to whom Villa had given money to buy arms. Ravel never delivered the weapons nor returned Villa's money.

Before the attack Villa told his men the reasons he had decided to attack this American town. He said the Carranza government had practically sold Mexico to the Americans. He also mentioned how the U.S. had been given the power to name three Mexican cabinet members. However, all this meant very little to Villa's illiterate soldiers.

One of Villa's top officer's, Pablo Lopez put it in plain terms. "We want revenge against the Americans," he yelled out. Lopez said the U.S. was to blame for their defeat at Agua Prieta and Celaya. He accused the Americans of allowing the Carrancistas to travel across U.S. land to reinforce their garrison.

Villa added another serious accusation, saying that the U.S. had sold them defective weapons and ammunition (Sam Ravel Incident). The biggest surprise though, was the terrible act that had occurred in El Paso just two days earlier. According to reports from the time, the following was standard practice. Some 20 Mexicans had been arrested by the local police and they had been soaked with kerosene to delouse them. An unknown person then set fire to the men. It was never proven whether the fire was an accident or not. However, all 20 Mexicans were burned alive. After hearing this story, Villa's soldiers were now ready to fight the entire American army.

Wire tower in town

During the raid it is said that Villa had stayed on the Mexican side of the border with a small group of his men. Meanwhile his raiders were looking for Sam Ravel, but never found him. He had already left town on a scheduled appointment with his dentist, in El Paso.

This clock while hanging in the railroad station was shot by one of Villa's men at 4:11 am.

In January 1916, Villa kidnapped 18 Americans from a Mexican train and slaughtered them.

Under the white paper in the top left corner is a bullet hole from one of the Villistas.

The Sam Ravel Incident is said as follows he sold defective weapons and ammunition to Villa. The munitions had very little gun powder which led to many Villistas being killed in battle.

A guest of the hotel tried to escape in this car but was shot multiple times by the Villistas.

Another possible reason for the attack was in 1913, Mexico was in a bloody civil war that brought the ruthless general Victoriano Huerta to power. American President Woodrow Wilson despised the new regime, referring to it as a "government of butchers," and provided active military support to a challenger, Venustiano Carranza. Unfortunately, when Carranza won power in 1914, he also proved a disappointment and Wilson supported yet another rebel leader, Pancho Villa. A wily, charismatic, peasant-born leader, Villa joined with Emiliano Zapata to keep the spirit of rebellion alive in Mexico and harass the Carranza government. A year later, though, Wilson decided Carranza had made enough steps towards democratic reform to merit official American support, and President Wilson abandoned Villa.

Bullet holes in the driver's door.

President Wilson ordered General John Pershing to lead 6,000 American troops into Mexico and capture Villa. Reluctantly, Carranza agreed to allow the U.S. to invade Mexican territory. For nearly two years, Pershing and his soldiers chased the elusive Villa on horseback, in automobiles, and with airplanes, (the first time planes were used but they had problems with the altitude being about 4000 feet high). The American troops had several bloody skirmishes with the rebels, but Pershing was never able to find, engage or capture Villa. Finally losing patience with the American military presence in his nation, Carranza withdrew permission for the occupation. Pershing returned home in early 1917, and three months later left for Europe as the head of the American Expeditionary Force of World War I. Pershings efforts did however convince Pancho Villa to never again attack American citizens or territory.

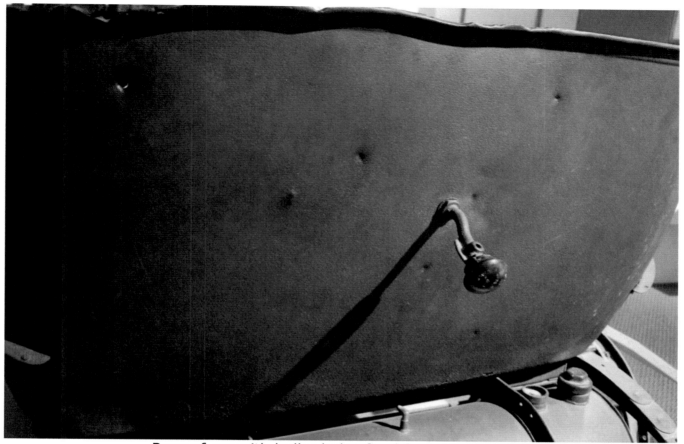

Rear of car with bullet holes fired from Villa's men.

Troopers found 67 dead Villistas "in the camp and town and burned the bodies [along with dead horses] the following day," said Lieutenant Lucas. "It is impossible to say what the Mexican casualties were, but they must have been heavy because the mesquite was full of them. Few of their wounded could have survived." The 13th Cavalry also seized several prisoners, hanging them from the gallows. The soldiers also discovered that many of the Villistas were 14- to 16-year-old kids.

Mural of Pancho Villa on a house in Chihuahua

About General Pancho Villa

Pancho Villa was born Doroteo Arango on June 5, 1878 to a family of impoverished sharecroppers who worked land belonging to the wealthy and powerful López Negrete family in the state of Durango. Pancho Villa's baptism name was José Doroteo Arango Arámbula.

According to legend, when young Doroteo caught one of the López Negrete clan trying to rape his younger sister Martina, he shot him in the foot and fled to the mountains. There he joined a band of outlaws and quickly through his bravery and ruthlessness became a leader. He earned good money as a bandit, and gave some if it back to the poor, which earned him a reputation of being a kind of Robin Hood.

Statue of General Pancho Villa meeting General Pershing of the US Army in Palomas, NM.

Statue of Pancho Villa in Palomas, NM

Statue of Pancho Villa in Palomas, NM

Pancho Villa Rides in Palomas, NM

Even though Pancho Villa had a macho-man image, he never drank alcohol. During the revolution, he allowed his men to drink, but he himself never did until late in his life after his 1920 peace with Alvaro Obregon. Many of Pancho Villa's men were Yaqui Indians (known as Las Cucarachas) who were very fond of smoking "motas" (marijuana cigarettes). It is said that the term marijuana originated with Villa's soldiers particularly the female camp followers who were known as soldaderas.

Villa was Governor of Chihuahua in 1913-1914. Villa showed that he had a knack for public administration. He sent his men to help harvest crops, ordered the repair of railways and telegraph lines and imposed a ruthless code of law and order which even applied to his own troops.

Villa commanded the most feared cavalry in the world at the time, he himself was an outstanding horseman who personally rode into battle with his men. He was so often on horseback during the Mexican Revolution that he earned the nickname "the Centaur of the North".

Statue of Pancho Villa in Mexico

Artwork about Pancho Villa on the base of his statue in Palomas NM

Villa personally killed many men on the battlefield and off of it. There were some jobs, however, that even he found too repulsive to do. Fortunately, he had Rodolfo Fierro, a sociopathic hit man who was fiercely loyal and absolutely fearless. According to legend, Fierro once shot a man dead just to see if he would fall forward or backward.

Artwork from the famous photo about pancho Villa sitting in the presidential chair (with Emiliano Zapata on his left) on the base of his statue in Palomas NM

Villa had no ambitions to be President of Mexico. He wanted the revolution to triumph in order to unseat Dictator Porfirio Diaz and he was a big supporter of Francisco Madero. After Madero's death, Villa never wholeheartedly supported any other presidential candidates. He hoped someone acceptable would come along so that he, Villa, could serve as a high-ranking military officer.

Pancho Villa had this mausoleum built in Chihuahua. Villa wanted to be intered there when he died. He was never buried there he was buried in Parral, Chihuahua where his body was stolen and decapitated. The headless body was recovered and reintered in Mexico City at the Monument of the Revolutionaries where other heroes of the revolution are buried.

Mausoleum that Pancho Villa built in Chihuahua Mexico.

Famous wanted poster

Pancho Villa was aware of how important press coverage was to his cause. It is said he even delayed an attack on Ciudad Juarez to avoid conflicting with the World Series.

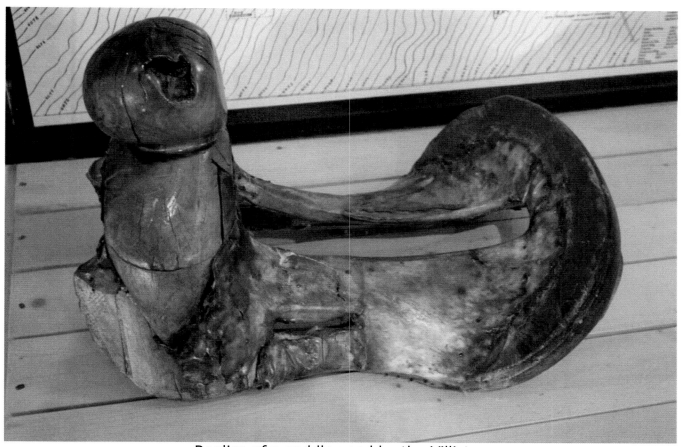

Replica of a saddle used by the Villistas

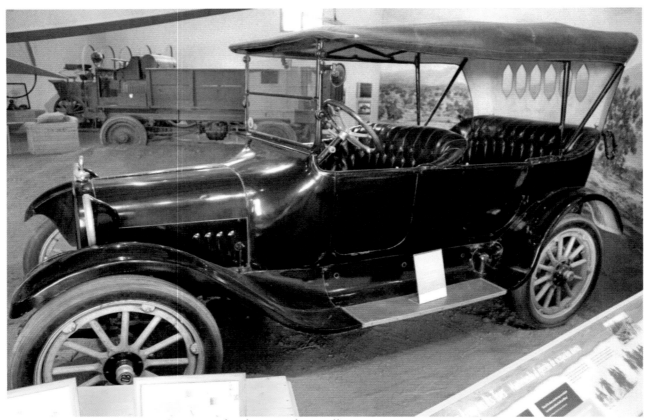

Car in which Pancho Villa was assassinated.

After helping remove Carranza from power in 1920, Villa agreed to retire from politics. His enemies assassinated him in 1923. On Friday, 20 July 1923, Villa was killed while visiting Parral. Villa was usually accompanied by his entourage of Dorados (his bodyguards), but had gone into the town without them on that day, taking only a few associates with him. He went to pick up a consignment of gold from the local bank with which to pay his Canutillo ranch staff. While driving back through the city in his black 1919 Dodge touring car, Villa passed by a school, and a pumpkin-seed vendor ran toward his car and shouted "Viva Villa!" This was a signal to a group of seven riflemen who then appeared in the middle of the road and fired more than 40 shots into the automobile. In the fusillade, nine dumdum bullets, normally used for hunting big game, hit Villa in the head and upper chest, killing him instantly.

The Jeffery Armored Car No.1 was developed by the Thomas B. Jeffery Company in Kenosha, Wisconsin 1915. The armored car No.1 was used in by General John Pershing's 1916 Pancho Villa Expedition in Columbus, New Mexico for training. Pancho Villa was far into Mexico at that time and there are no records on its use in fighting.

The Jeffery Armored Car No.1 located at Pancho Villa State Park Columbus, NM.

Inside of the Jeffery Armored Car No.1

Pancho Villas home in Chihuahua, NM

Pancho Villa once had 122 bars of silver ingots from a train robbery along with a Wells Fargo employee who was his hostage. Pancho Villa forced Wells Fargo to help him sell the ingots for cash that could be used quicker than silver ingots.

Courtyard in the Pancho Villa home which was given to Mexico after his wife Luz's death and then turned into a historical revolutionary museum that is maintained by the Military.

Villa once signed a contract with Mutual Film Company, of New York for $25,000 dollars for the exclusive rights to the revolution. The Mutual Film Company provided boots, fancy guns, and confederate uniforms to the front row so Pancho's soldiers would look better on the big screen. Mutual Films filmed the bloody battles where Villa defeated the Federal forces at Gomez Palacio, Torreon, and Zacatecas.

Photo of a Villista

   Pancho Villas soldiers, mainly serving in the Division del Norte (Northern Division). Formed part of the Maderista forces, and later fought in opposition to the Huerta and Carranza governments, the Villistas later formed a spatially isolated alliance with the Zapatistas, who remained in Morelos. Villa's men were mostly made up of vaquero and charro caudillos, rancheros, shopkeepers, miners, migrant farm workers, unemployed workers, railway workers, and Maderista bureaucrats, who seized haciendas and fought for an undefined socialism. Adolfo Gilly wrote that Villismo, though fighting for land redistribution and justice, did not challenge capitalist relations as previously set down during the Porfirio era, but was merely an outgrowth of the bourgeois state-oriented revolution of Madera.

Hat worn by Pancho Villa

Villa's death mask was hidden at the Radford School in El Paso, Texas, until the 1980s, when it was sent to the Historical Museum of the Mexican Revolution in Chihuahua. Other museums have ceramic and bronze representations that do not match this mask.

In total the United States had a force of more than 10,000 men, 9,000 horses, and 20 odd Villistas prisoners crossed the border at Columbus, NM. The final cost of the manhunt was $130 million dollars.

About the Author
Willie Ortiz is an avid wildlife, nature and travel photographer. He has traveled the world to view and photograph animals in their natural habitat. When the natural habitat is almost impossible Willie is a patron of animal rehabilitation and education centers. Willie's photography can be seen on the Your Shot by National Geographic and Flickr. Animals of Belize Willies first book truly shows the passion he has for protecting wildlife though education. Willie Ortiz is originally from the Bronx and currently resides on the Treasure Coast of Florida.

Made in the USA
Middletown, DE
23 April 2023